Forex Trading Top 5 Strategies

The Ultimate Guide to Maximize Your Profit and Reduce Risks

Andrew C. Ellis

© Copyright 2018 by Andrew C. Ellis

All rights reserved.

The following eBook is reproduced below with the goal of providing information that is as accurate and as reliable as possible. Regardless, purchasing this eBook can be seen as consent to the fact that both the publisher and the author of this book are in no way experts on the topics discussed within, and that any recommendations or suggestions made herein are for entertainment purposes only. Professionals should be consulted as needed before undertaking any of the action endorsed herein.

This declaration is deemed fair and valid by both the American Bar Association and the Committee of Publishers Association and is legally binding throughout the United States.

Furthermore, the transmission, duplication or reproduction of any of the following work, including precise information, will be considered an illegal act, irrespective whether it is done electronically or in print. The legality extends to creating a secondary or tertiary copy of the work or a recorded copy and is only allowed with express written consent of the Publisher. All additional rights are reserved.

The information in the following pages is broadly considered to be a truthful and accurate account of facts, and as such any inattention, use or misuse of the information in question by the reader will render any resulting actions solely under their purview. There are no scenarios in which the publisher or the original author of this work can be in any fashion deemed liable for any hardship or damages that may befall them after undertaking information described herein.

Additionally, the information found on the following pages is intended for informational purposes only and should thus be considered, universal. As befitting its nature, the information presented is without assurance regarding its continued validity or interim quality. Trademarks that mentioned are done without written consent and can in no way be considered an endorsement from the trademark holder.

Table of Contents

Chapter 1: The Basics of Forex 7

Chapter 2: Bolly Band Bounce Trading 11

Chapter 3: Forex Overlapping Fibonacci Strategy 23

Chapter 4: Trading Forex in Fractal Terms 35

Chapter 5: Bladerunner Reversal Strategy 47

Chapter 6: London Hammer Forex Strategy 59

Conclusion 69

Description 71

Introduction

Congratulations on downloading your personal copy of *Forex Trading Top 5 Strategies: The Ultimate Guide to Maximize Your Profit and Reduce Risks.* Thank you for doing so.

The following chapters will discuss some of the many things that you can do to start trading Forex.

You will discover how important it is to try different things until something works for you.

The final chapter will explore the benefits that come along with Forex and how you can use it to trade, make money and be able to live a comfortable life.

There are plenty of books on this subject on the market. Thanks again for choosing this one! Every effort was made to ensure it is full of as much useful information as possible. Please enjoy!

Chapter 1:

The Basics of Forex

In its simplest form, the idea behind Forex is that people who deal in it trade the money that they have for money that is from a different country so that they can make money on it. They take advantage of the exchange rate that is determined in the terms of the trade and that changes the way that they can make money on the trades that they are doing. It is a way for people to just make money from the exchange rates.

Forex is simply an abbreviation of foreign exchange. It simply means that the trades are trading money back and forth between two (or more) markets where they are able to get the most amount of money possible. While you may have thought that stocks, bonds, and other types of trading were the most popular, Forex is actually the most popular form of trading.

Each day, there is over 5 trillion dollars that are traded in the Forex market. That is between all of the different markets that participate and all of the ones that are around the world, and it has enabled people the chance to make sure that they are going to be able to get the best experience possible with Forex. When you trade with Forex, you will give yourself the best chance possible at being able to make more money and being able to profit from the money that you already have.

Some people who are just getting started with trading or who do not know what they want to do with it yet may be intimidated by the different aspects of Forex trading. Just because there is such a high rate that is traded in Forex on a daily basis doesn't mean that you can't do it too and get the same benefits out of it.

The biggest thing that you need to remember when you are Forex trading is that you will need to start out small. Don't trade thousands of dollars when you are first getting started so that you don't have to worry about losing a lot of money. The less money that you choose to invest, the lower your risk will be when trading.

It is a good idea to always follow the proven successful strategies. The strategies that are outlined in this book are the most popular and are the ones nearly all of the people who trade Forex use. The chapters outline the type of attitude that you need to trade using each of the strategies along with the benefits and downsides of each of them. It will help you to make the right decision on what strategy you are going to be able to use for your Forex trading experience. You can make sure that you are getting the best trade opportunities possible when you decide to use one of these strategies for your Forex trading experience.

Chapter 2:
Bolly Band Bounce Trading

Understanding the way to trade with bands is different than if you were going to be able to trade using the strategies that are normally used for different types of foreign exchange trades. This is because the band trading strategy is something that will help you to have a better time with the options that you do have. It is a trading strategy that is great for beginners, but it will also help people understand the way to do Forex trading so that they can make sure that they are doing everything the right way.

If you are just getting started with trading, or more specifically Forex trading, you can make sure that you are giving yourself the best start possible by doing bolly band trading.

If you are going to use the bolly ban bounce trading strategy, you can see that there is a limit on the time that a price can move around. Unlike range trading where the price is able to move around as much as the market does, bolly band bounce prevents the market from having any effect on the way that the short-term time limit is able to work with the different things that are going on in your specific trade.

The behavior that is observed in the market is easier to understand when you are looking at it in a sense of the bolly band bounce trading. It can change based on the different aspects that are predicted in the market, but it will have less of an influence on the things that are going on in the market. They can expand and contract based on the different trading options that people are putting into them. The band part of the terminology relates to something like a rubber band that can come forward and then bounce back relatively easy. If you look at the statistics of bolly band bounce trades, it is clear to see that they expand and contract on a regular basis.

Unlike the less moral options with Forex trading that some people choose to use, bolly band bounce trades are able to be used no matter what type of market that you are going to use. There are several steps that you can use to be able to get involved in this type of market, and each of the steps are easy for you to follow.

1. Determination

The first step that you will need to take with bolly band bounce trading is the determination factor. You will not be able to get any results unless you are able to determine what is going to happen with it. Once you are able to actually determine the Forex trade that you are going to be able to make, you will be able to make a better chance at creating a higher income for yourself.

2. One Side, Mid-Band

As you are looking at the trends for your Forex trade and the bolly band bounce, you want to look out for the mid-band to be off to one side. It is more on one side, and that appears to be with the past trend that you are looking at. When you are working to make sure that you can get the best Forex option for yourself and with the trades that you have, you will need to figure out what is going to work best for you. The best way to do this is by making sure that the one side, mid-band idea is going to help you with the options that you have in your Forex trade. It will enable you to find the right amount of money and the right choice when it comes to your trades.

3. Signal a Turn

There will always be a turn in your trade. This is the point where things change for the trade. If the constant exchange rate going up is something that you are looking for with your Forex trade, keep in mind that it is not always going to continue to go up. There will be a turn and you will need to be prepared for the signal that comes along with it. By understanding this, you can keep in mind that you will be able to see the exchange rate go down (or go up). Keep in mind that you will need to try different things when a turn happens so watch out for that signal.

4. Confirmation

The confirmation step of bolly band bounce trading is that you will need to be sure that what you are truly getting out of the experience is a good trade. If you want to make sure that you are getting the best experience possible and the highest trade exchange rate, you will need to confirm the amount of the trade so that you can figure out what your profit is going to be.

Once you have made the confirmation and you know the amount of money that you stand to make, you can truly benefit from everything that is included with bolly band bounce trading. You will be on your way to a profit.

5. Stop Loss

No matter what type of trading you are doing, whether it is Forex trading, investing or any other type of trade, you should make sure that you have a stop loss in place so that you can make the best decision possible. The stop loss will prevent you from having a problem with your trades and will also give you the chance to see that there is so much more to trading than losing money. The stop loss will keep you from losing money up to a certain amount and will give you the options that you need to make sure that you are getting the best experience possible.

If you want to make sure that you are protected, a stop loss is the only way that you are able to do so. It can help save you from having major problems that are often associated with unregulated trading and with the way that many people lose money just from starting out in their trade career.

6. Profit

The amount that you profit on your Forex trades will depend on the exchange rate that you have found. It will also depend on the amount of money that you need to be able to put into it. In general, those who use bolly band bounce trading strategies are not able to profit quite as much as the people who use other strategies. This is likely due to the fact that the risk is not as high with bolly band bounce. The lower the risk is when it comes to the trades that you have, the lower the rewards are going to be for you.

Keep that in mind when you are trading but understand that the lower risk is going to be the best option for you as you get started with the Forex trade options.

Attitude

The right attitude will always be able to suit your needs when you are trading in Forex. Having the right mindset and the right goals for your trades is something that will set you apart from others who do not know what they are doing or who want to be able to try different things without taking into account all of the problems that can come with trades that they are doing.

Having a new trader attitude while you are doing bolly band bounce trading is one of the best things that you can do. It is something that seems like it was perfectly optimized for people who want to be able to get the true best experience out of trading, and it is something that is great for beginners.

When it comes to bolly band bounce trades, you do not really need a specific attitude to make it work the best way possible for you. That is one of the many reasons why it is good for beginners and a reason why most people who are just getting started should choose bolly band bounce trading.

If you are working through the different processes of trading and you keep that same beginner attitude for trading, you *will* have problems that you will have to deal with because of the things that are included with the different options that you have.

Always make sure that you are doing your best and that you are learning the right attitude.

It doesn't matter as much with bolly band bounce, but you will see major problems if you do the same thing with other Forex trade strategies.

Pros

The most obvious benefit that comes with bolly band bounce trading is that there is not a large margin for error with the options that are included with it. This can be a good thing and a bad thing depending on what you want to do, but for the most part, it is a positive aspect of this type of strategy.

When you are just getting started, the bolly band bounce trading strategy will be the best option for you. This is because it will give you the chance to be able to do more with the money that you have and not need to worry about the problems that come with losing a lot of money or having very high risks that are associated with the trades that you do. While you are working on your trades, consider the bolly band bounce strategy as one of the easiest options to deal with in Forex.

There are many positive sides that come with bolly band bounce strategy, but keep in mind that you are doing what you can to be able to get a small amount of profit.

Another great benefit that is included is that you will be able to see the different trends. There are charts, graphs, and many other options that are included with bolly band bounce trading. You can see all of the rest of the trade options that are associated with Forex when you do bolly band bounce trading.

Essentially, it is a strategy that you can use to help yourself get started. It connects you with the other types of strategies and gives you the chance to enter into Forex trading without too much of a risk that you will have to deal with.

Cons

The biggest problem that comes along with bolly band bounce strategy is that you will not be able to make as much money as if you were doing other types of strategies. It can be difficult to get to a certain ceiling of money from your trades, and once you hit that ceiling, it will be almost impossible for you to overcome it and make things better with your trades. The Forex sector is complicated and has many different facets. Bolly band bounce only focuses on a small portion of those trades, and it can be hard to get past that while you are trading.

Keep all of this in mind while you are thinking about the trades that are available and what you can do with them.

Bolly band bounce trading is not the end of the line for those who are hoping to become good at Forex. In fact, it is just the beginning. Use bolly band bounce trading to get started with Forex trading and then move on to another type of trade strategy so that you can make sure that you are going to get what you need out of the different options that are included in your experience. It will allow you to just enter into the trade opportunities without much of a risk to yourself.

Chapter 3:

Forex Overlapping Fibonacci Strategy

After you have become familiar with Forex trading and you start to get more involved in it, you will find that some of the strategies are more complicated than others. There are many different strategies that you can use, but keep in mind that not all of them are created equal. You may struggle to figure out what is going to work for you and what you will be able to do with the strategies, but if you always work to make sure that you are doing the right thing with your strategy, you will have a great chance at being able to include all of the trade options in with your Forex trades. You won't have to worry about the major problems that come with other types of trades so that you can focus more on the sequences and on the strategies that are all included with your different options.

With Fibonacci sequences, traders need to learn how to combine the past that the trade has had with the future that is included with the different areas located in the options that they have to be able to try new things. If you can see the exchange rate that is close to what you have had in the past, the chances are that the Fibonacci sequence is going to work great for you and with what you have available for the sources that you are using.

Most traders will not even attempt to use the overlapping Fibonacci trade pattern until they feel like they have mastered Fibonacci on its own and with the different directions that will help them to get what they need out of the various trade strategies. You can count on the trade amounts to work for you if you are using overlapping Fibonacci but only if you use it in the right way.

The steps to using Fibonacci overlapping trades are somewhat complicated but they can be easily done if you have the right trade options available for yourself and if you are doing more with the options that are included in your trade budget. Make sure that you know the steps and that you follow them so that you can make more money off of the trades that you have and with the various Forex exchange rates that you are going to use.

1. Learn Fibonacci

Once you have learned about Forex and what you want to be able to do with it, you can then learn the Fibonacci sequences that are going to work for you. This is the pattern that is included with trades – it is an up and down pattern, but one that does not have major falls and rises to it. Instead, it is just something that stays along the same lines as the other things that are going on within it. Use the mathematical sequence to learn what the exchange rates are going to be and how they will work for you.

2. Extended Fibonacci

As the Fibonacci sequence grows in size and you work to find out what the exchange rate is going to mean for your investment and with the trades that you are doing, you can try different things with Fibonacci. It will also give you the chance to be able to increase the various options that you have within your trade amounts. Always keep that in mind so that you don't have to worry about what is going to happen when the exchange rate expands along with Fibonacci.

3. Retracted Fibonacci

Opposite to how the extended Fibonacci works, you will be able to see major differences in the rates with retracted Fibonacci. This is something that can be complicated and something that will show that the rates are dropping. If you see this, you should know that your exchange rate is going to be lower, and you will not be able to truly get the best experience out of it if you do it in that way. There are many new options that are included with retracted Fibonacci so that you can try new things and you can do more with what you have in your Forex trades.

4. Combine Together

The best part about overlapping Fibonacci is that you can combine the retracted and the extended Fibonacci sequences. These will allow you to try new things and do much more with the options that you have. It will also allow you to learn about the profits that you can make through Fibonacci. If you are just going to use one of the initial ideas behind the sequence, there is no point in doing the overlapping technique. Instead, you can just use a singular approach to Fibonacci and use that for the trades that you have.

5. Watch for Candlesticks

With some Forex trading strategies, candlesticks that appear in the patterns of trade terms are good and can mean that you are making money. With the overlapping Fibonacci sequences, though, candlesticks are not a good thing. They can mean that the amount of your exchange rate is going to plummet or that there are other major problems with the trade approach. A candlestick, when you are looking at trends, is an upshot of the pattern that comes on quickly after low points in the pattern, and it can be problematic if you are going to try and make sure that you are getting the true best trade experience from Forex.

6. Create Profit

The Fibonacci sequence and the subsequent overlapping sequences are all in place to help you profit from the things that you are doing with your Forex trades. You will need to make sure that you are doing things the right way and that you are getting the best experience possible from the trades that you do. It can be complicated to get profits from overlapping Fibonacci, but doing this will give you the chance to be able to add more to the options that you have.

Profit is the most important part of any trade, so when you learn how the sequence works and the right way to use the strategy, you can see how profitable your Forex trades will be. The profits that are included give you the option to do more with your sequences and with the rest of the way that things work within your own trade experience.

Having a huge profit is not something that will happen if you are using other strategies, but you can start to collect on bigger profits when you are using the Fibonacci sequence to make things better for yourself and with the different situations that you are in.

7. Reinvest

Always put the money back into trading. Your profits will not mean anything if you are not able to reinvest your money back in. Watch for the exchange rates and see how they change according to the different market factors. You may be surprised to learn that you are not going to get the best options possible from your trades if you don't reinvest. Always keep an eye on the exchange rates and do everything that you can to get your money put in when they are good.

It is often complicated to learn the way that trade strategies work. As one of the most complicated strategies, Fibonacci overlapping sequences can be hard to understand. You will need to make sure that you are prepared for this and that you are doing everything that you can to learn about it. As you dive more deeply into trading, you will find that each strategy has its own approach, and you will need to figure that out as you learn more about them. If you have the right outlook and the right amount of time to wait on a profit, you can truly make a lot of money from the overlapping Fibonacci.

Your Attitude

The attitude that you take when you are using overlapping Fibonacci should be one of patience. You will need to have a lot of patience. Not only does it take a long time to get where you want to be with the sequences and the trade amounts that you have, but it can also take a long time for you to figure out the right way to add different options to your experience. Always remember that you will be able to do more if you have the right amount of patience with overlapping Fibonacci.

It is a good idea to take your time, learn about it and figure out how you are going to use the strategy with Forex. You should do this as a type of practice before you actually begin to use Forex. You don't know the type of help that you can get from using Forex so there are many problems that will come along with the trades that you make and with the different options that you have with the Fibonacci overlapping experience.

If you want to make sure that you have the right attitude, consider the amount of time that it is going to take to get the profits that you want. The profits are not going to come quickly and you will need to think about that before you try to make the right decision on your trade experience. An attitude that allows you to be prepared for all of the different things that can happen during your trade time will give you the best experience possible and will also allow you to try new things with the options that you have set out to use for trading.

Pros

There are many pros that come along with using the overlapping Fibonacci strategy to make your trades better for yourself. It is a great way to ensure that you are going to get the options that you need and that you are going to be able to include everything that you want with your trading experience.

By looking at the different pros that are associated with overlapping Fibonacci, you can see that it will be a great choice in some instances.

One of the biggest pros that overlapping Fibonacci will offer you is that it provides very high profits if you have the chance to wait. Since the experience is going through both extension and retraction, it will be much easier for you to figure out what you can do to include the many options in your own experience. It will also allow you to profit more with just a small amount of money. The rewards that come from overlapping Fibonacci are often worth the hard work and patience that has to go into the trading experience. You will be able to enjoy the benefits of overlapping Fibonacci and take as much advantage of it as possible.

Cons

While we have already learned that the biggest downside is the amount of time that it will take you to start profiting, there are also some other downsides that you will need to take into account. For example, the complications that come along with overlapping Fibonacci can be tiresome and can cause you to want to be able to try something else. They are difficult to be able to experience, and you may not want to get the options that you want.

As you learn more about your Forex options and the trades that you are doing, overlapping Fibonacci will also have some other downsides to it. Since the rewards are bigger with this type of trade, it is easy to see that the risk is also much greater. You can take that risk if you are willing to, or you can try new things that will bring you similar rewards but not as much of a risk.

If the market does not swing the same way or if your Fibonacci does not expand after it retracts, you will not be able to make as much of a profit from it and you may start to lose money on the things that you have already set out to invest in.

Chapter 4:

Trading Forex in Fractal Terms

While the other types of Forex trading strategies focus on trying to use outside sources to be able to figure out the right type of trades, fractal trading involves using the portions – or fractals – of Forex to be able to make a difference in the amount that you can spend and what you can do to be able to make money from the trades that you are participating in. It is a good idea to learn more about fractals before you start to use them. While they can be a beginner type of trading option if you are planning to deal in Forex, you will still need to learn some basics about the fractals and how you can actually start to make money from them.

Fractals in Investing

Most of the time, people will use fractals to be able to make a difference in the type of trading that they are doing. Fractals are a mathematical term that is often used in advanced math ideologies, but they can also be applied to other situations. For example, fractals can be a part of a market, and they can be applied to different situations within the market. Many traders, though, think of fractals as patterns that come up over and over again. They can help to predict what is going to happen to the pattern of the market, and they will determine where there will be bigger spikes in a market of chaos.

To help yourself identify a fractal when you are trading within the Forex market, you will need to make sure that it meets more than one of the following criteria:

- Turning point that is different from what you would normally add to different situations. It will look bearish, or it will be more toward the positive side of the market. The pattern will show that there are three highs. Two of the highs will be about average. The third high will lie in between the other two and will be much larger.

- A turning point that is opposite of the first one. A bull turning point will be a pattern using the low points of the graph, and they will look the same as the bearish ones except they will be reversed. There will be three low points. In between the two low points that are the same size or close to it, there will be a very low point that is at least double the size of the other two low points.

- There will be more than five points that are on the bars of the graph. This is something that is necessary to be able to figure out where the graph stands and what it is able to do in the different parts of the trading sequence. If you are going to use fractals for Forex trading, you must make sure that all of the bars are in the same graph and that they are all going in different directions that will help to determine whether or not it is a true fractal.

There is a chance that you will see all of the points that are listed as the criteria in a fractal graph, but that is not always the case. The more likely case is that you will be able to only see two of them. You can now see why it is important to make sure that there are more than one of the criteria in the graph. If there were only one, it would simply be a graph that is showing the different things that are happening in a market. Having the other factors included with it and having the ability to see that they are all in that same situation will make it easier for you to recognize that it is, in fact, a fractal.

In Trading

You should not rely only on fractals to do the trades that you want to do. It is a good idea to try different things and to use other identifying factors to make it easier for you to find the fractals that you have in different types of trade situations. It is best to use two types of strategies together, but if you are going to use just one, the fractal strategy is a great way to get started and will give you some of the most accurate readings.

There are issues that can come about from trading with using only fractals, but these are mainly minor issues. As long as you are working to make sure that you are checking your trades, you will be able to use fractals successfully. The use of another method in combination with fractals is to simply check and make sure that you are doing the trades the right way. If you don't check and you can't figure out the right way to be able to do things with the Forex trading that you are doing, you could risk missing out on good trade opportunities. Always make sure that you are doing what you can to be able to get the best trade possible with fractal trading opportunities.

Remember...

Fractals are not perfect. They are a great way to see the different aspects of trading and what it can mean to you, but there is no way to guarantee that using them will help you to make money. It is always a good idea to try new things and to be sure that you are using each of these things to give yourself the help that you need. When you are trading Forex in fractals, you should keep these things in mind:

- There is always a lag with fractals. They are not in real time, and you will not be able to use them to get an accurate reading of what is going on in the market *right now.* Unlike the other methods that allow you to see the way that the market is going, fractals give you the option to be able to see what has happened in the past and nothing more. For that reason, you can use them to confirm what happened on the market. If you want to see whether a reversal really happened, fractals are your best option for that.
- You will need to set parameters for the fractals that you are figuring out. If you set the parameters so that they are a long time and so that there is a lot of room between them, you will be able to get a better reading of what is going on with the fractals. Always keep in mind that you will need to set those parameters. Whether you set them for a long time or a short time, all depends on what you

want to be able to do with your trade options.
- Plot your fractals in multiple frames – always. Try to figure out different time frames that you can use and then put the fractals in. It is a good idea to then bring the two of the time periods together. This way, you can see what happened independently in each of the time periods so that you can make sure that you are getting the best experience possible. If you can see that the two time periods are separate from one another, you will be able to see that there are different options depending on the time that you are a part of.
- Don't use the fractals on their own. You can use them for a short period of time if you are just checking on them and trying to figure out what you can do with them, but if you are going to use them for actual statistics or to base your trades off of, you will need to use some other method of trading strategy. Consider using the London Hammer method to help you get to the point where you will be able to use the statistics for actual trading.

Attitude

Keep in mind that it is important that you work to make sure that you know that there are a lot of steps to fractal trading. Not only do you need to worry about the fractals and what they mean for the Forex trades that you are making, but you will also need to make sure that you have another method that is ready and prepared for you to be able to cross check the work that you have done. If you can make sure that you are cross checking everything, you will have a much easier time with the fractal method.

Know that you are not always going to be able to be successful even when you use something like fractal trading. There is a good chance that, even though you are looking at the fractals and the different options that are included in your Forex trades, you will not be able to succeed. Be prepared to do poorly with the fractals that you have, and it will not be as disappointing when you do not reach the profit margin that you were hoping for.

Pros

There are many positive aspects of using fractals. One of the best things about using them is that you can make sure that you are getting the most accurate and up-to-date information on the trends that have happened on the market in the time period that you put into the parameters or guidelines that you have set up for the fractals. It is a good idea to recognize that you can do more and learn more with the different options that there are available to you in fractal Forex trading. By making sure that you can add all of the different time periods in, you are giving yourself the advantage.

Other benefits that come along with fractal trading is that you can see detailed reports, you can add additional information, and you can use any combination of your favorite trade strategies to figure out what has happened in the past. Doing all of these things will give you a great experience and will also give you the best options possible for your trading experience. You can also benefit from the way that things are done in fractals by including all of the different pieces that you will put together for the total trade experience. If you know how to look at your Forex trades in fractals, you can also help yourself predict what is going to happen with the trades in the future. No matter where you are trading or what you are trading with, fractals can help you get a better picture of what the trades mean in different situations.

Cons

The biggest problem that comes with fractals is that you will not get the most accurate information when you look at fractals alone. The fractal information that you have with your trading and the terms of the trades in the past can all be decided based on the information that you get from fractals, but without another source, you won't be able to see what they are doing or how that is going to affect your trades. You also won't be able to see whether or not they are doing the same in real time as what they were in the past. If you want to be sure that you are getting the most accurate information with fractals, you can use another trade strategy.

Aside from the fact that the fractal trading strategy is the only one that requires you to use another type of strategy in combination with it, it is a great option to have for the trades that you want to make. No matter what you are doing with your Forex or what you have planned to do with it in the future, fractals can give you a picture of the past with Forex so that you can know what to base your trade on. Knowing the past makes it easier to learn the patterns.

Chapter 5:

Bladerunner Reversal Strategy

With a bladerunner strategy, you will be able to accomplish many different things that come along with your trading of Forex. The pattern that is most commonly associated with Bladerunner strategy is one that has a steady stream of the same amount of trade exchanges, followed by a huge increase and then leveling out to slightly above the regular line of trades but still far below the big spike that you saw at the beginning. Opposite of that, with a reversed Bladerunner, you will see a steady stream of the same amount of trade prices throughout the line of different things. Then, you will see a large drop in it, and it will start to level out toward the end. This is an easy strategy to understand, but it can be somewhat difficult for you to try and predict what is going to happen with it in the future of the pattern that you created.

The Bladerunner in its originally form is simply a combination of two major strategies – bolly band and 20 EMA, which is not something that fits in with the other strategies. There are many different aspects to both of these trade strategies, but they are able to work together well with the reversed Bladerunner.

One thing that you will notice with the Bladerunner strategy is that you will need to pay attention to the polarity indicator to make sure that you are truly getting the best price and exchange rate possible. This is something that is important, and it will help you to figure out the right way to trade. You will need to know when the right time is to invest in the exchange rate. If you do it too soon, you may not get the best price possible. If you do it too late, you will miss out on the opportunity to buy it.

There are a few steps, though, that you can follow that fit the polarity indicator into them to give you the best chance possible at getting your Forex trade at the exact right time so that you can make sure that you will be able to get everything done in the way that you want.

1. Adjust the Trade

Before you even get started with the trades that you are going to do with the options that you have, you will need to make sure that you are adjusting your trade so that you can get the best experience possible and get the most out of the trade terms that you have. It will allow you the chance to see that you can do more and find out exactly how much money you are going to be able to make with what you have. If you know the right way to adjust your trade, you will give yourself the chance to cash in on the trade opportunities.

2. Learn the Polarity

There are many different types of polarity that you can find with Bladerunner reversal strategy. In general, if you find that the trade points are at one polar end or the other, the chances are that they will be a good trade for you to do. The exchange rate is indicated by the different trade terms and with all of the different amounts that the exchange rate is capable of creating for the options that you have. If you want to be able to reach the different amounts that are on the reversed Bladerunner strategy, you can make sure that you are doing so by always checking the polarity.

3. Create Terms

You should always make sure that you are creating your own terms for trades. These can be anything from the total amount that you are going to exchange to the point where you want to stop trading so that you can make the most amount of money possible. When you are working to create your own terms, it will give you a chance to completely customize the ideas that are behind the trades and the different options that they include with your Bladerunner reversal strategy.

4. Begin Trading

The easiest way to make money is to simply start trading. It is a good idea to have some sort of clue on what you are going to need to truly get started with the trade, but after you have learned as much as you can about it, you can just get started with trading. All you need to do is have some sort of income that you can use and then put that into the exchange rate. The amount that you spend when it comes to Forex trading and the different options that you have for your profits will help you to have a better time with the things that you choose to do.

5. Set Up Profit Beginning

You can begin to profit from your Forex trades as soon as you start doing them. If you are using your Bladerunner reversal strategy, all you need to do is look at the amount that you are going to put into it and see where it sits in relation to where it *should* sit according to the strategy. If you are going to put the money in, all you need to do is put it in and then exchange it for the total amount that you will begin to profit on.

6. Create a Stop Loss for Your Time

The stop loss is what will help you to make sure that you are not losing huge amounts of money to the Forex trades that you are doing. Stop losses essentially show that you will be able to do more with what you have and with the amount that you have put into it. If you put a stop loss in place on your Forex trades and you enforce the stop loss so that you can make your trades better, you will be able to save more money and you will not have to worry about what will happen if you invest over the amount that you wanted to invest.

7. Work with the Polarity

The polarity is almost always going to change depending on the different situations that you are in and the money that you have spent in these situations. Instead of trying to fight the polarity of the trade amount or work around it (which can eat up a huge amount of your time), you can work to be sure that you are getting the most out of the trading experience by going *with* the polarity. As the changes take effect, your polarity will also be able to change with the different things that you are doing.

8. Create More Trade Opportunities

As with everything that you do concerning Forex and the trading strategies that you are using, try to use the Bladerunner reversal strategy again and then make sure that you are providing the best opportunity to yourself. You need to always invest your profits back into the trades that you are doing. If you are constantly exchanging your profits and trying to make more money off of them, you will give yourself more opportunities to be able to create better profits for the options that you have.

It is always wise to consider the different aspects that come along with trades and the Forex industry. You will need to keep some things in mind while you are using the Bladerunner strategy. For example, just because you are using a strategy does not make the trade process foolproof. It is something that you must keep track of and something that you will constantly need to work at so that you are still profiting and are not losing money based on the different things that you are doing. By creating more opportunity for yourself, you will give the trades a better chance at being able to help you profit from them.

Attitude

With the bladerunner reversal idea of Forex trading, you should make sure that you are prepared with an attitude that understands there will be huge dips and rises in the amounts that you are trading. While you are looking at the patterns and using them to help yourself, you will be able to figure out the specific amounts and the different things that you can do with each of these. It is always a good idea to try and make sure that you are going to be able to use these to the best of your abilities. It is also a good decision to try new things and to know that the changes can have an effect on you.

If you want to get the most out of the Bladerunner reversal, your attitude will need to be one that is nonchalant. You will need to go with the ebbs and flows of the Bladerunner reversal so that you can make sure that you are prepared for the fact that there *will* be changes in your trades. There is no guarantee that you will get anything, but there is even less of a chance that you can get the exact trade amount that you were looking for with Bladerunner reversal.

Pros

There are several major benefits that come with using the bladerunner reversal strategy:

- Increased profits
- Bigger rewards for the risks that you take

- Lack of predictability – new and exciting opportunities with each trade
- Ability to change the way that you trade and the amount
- Visibility of the polarity of different things within the trading sector

While you are working to make sure that you can get the best opportunity possible for your trades, you will need to make sure that you are using the bladerunner reversal strategy in the right way. For some people, this means that they need to make sure that they are doing different trades and that they are going to be able to get the trade amount that they want with the options that they have. For others, it simply means that they will need to make sure that they can get the total amount back on the trades that they have created with the foreign exchange.

While the pros that come along with the Bladerunner reversal strategy are great for right now, they are something that you will need to figure out as you progress through the different aspects of trading. There will be times when you won't be able to get the best opportunities, and that can mean that you won't be able to learn how to change different things about the options in your trade sector. If you want to make the most amount of money possible, you need to carefully weigh the pros of the Bladerunner reversal strategy with the cons of it.

Cons

The cons that come along with the Bladerunner reversal strategy are often enough to have people choosing *not* to go with this strategy for the different things that they are going to be able to do. It is not only something that you will need to think carefully about but also something that you will need to do if you want to be able to make a lot of money that comes from the options that you have and with the Forex trading terms that you have created for yourself.

If you are going to use the cons in any way other than to see what the differences can be, you should always make sure that you know what they are. Some of the cons that come along with Bladerunner reversal strategy include not being able to see anything other than the polarity, losing money because you didn't know that it was going to drop and not understanding the pattern. It is also important to note that the pattern is sporadic and that it does not constantly repeat itself in the same way that other strategies do, so you have to be careful about predicting the things that are going to happen. If you try too hard to figure out what is going to happen with the trades, the chances are that you will miss out on them.

Chapter 6:

London Hammer Forex Strategy

When you think about the different types of trades and London Hammer comes up, the chances are that you think about the hammer coming down on the trades and the ability to bring your hopes and dreams crashing down with the different things that the trades bring. That is not the case, though. The London Hammer is actually one of the best Forex trading strategies that there is available to people. If you know what you are doing with your Forex trading career, you are confident in your ability to predict the patterns that are going to happen, and you want to make sure that you are doing what you can, you will be able to truly enjoy the London

Hammer strategy. This is something that will allow you to make sure that you are getting the best experience possible and that you will be able to make a lot of money from the options that you have.

It is always a good idea to make sure that you are getting what you can out of your trading strategies. Make sure that you are working toward the different options that are included with the Forex trades that you are doing and that each of the trades that you make will give you the options that you need to be able to succeed.

The London Hammer is made up of a large number of candlesticks. You may recognize the candlestick as an easy concept that has a huge spike in the amount of the trade followed by somewhat of a plateau, another small spike, and then another plateau. It then drops off back to where it was before the first spike or even lower than that. This happens several times in each group of the London hammer, and you will be able to see that it changes often. There are large spikes of many different candlesticks, and there are also smaller spikes that have candlesticks in them but are not quite as influential as the rest of the larger spikes in the amount that has changed.

You can get started with the London Hammer strategy relatively easy.

You will need to make sure that you do several different things:

- Learn how the strategy works – Just because there are big dips does not mean that the price is always going to go up. It could actually drop, which would be detrimental to your trade amount and to the different things that you have done with your Forex trade. There are many different options that you can include with your London hammer, so make sure that you are applying them as best as you can.
- Record the Forex trades – You will want to keep track of the trades that you are going to be able to do with the different options that you have. For some people, this will mean that they will simply need to write a few things

down. For others, they will have to write down a lot of information regarding the trades that they have set up for themselves. No matter what you are doing with your trades or with the Forex options that you have, you should make sure that you are prepared for the scattered dips and falls.

- Know it will rise – The London hammer will always rise back up from a dip. When this is the strategy that you are using, you will be able to notice right away that it is a rise-and-fall type of strategy. It is something that people rely on and something that will help you to have an easier time figuring out how much money you are going to make. Keep the rises and falls in mind but don't get too discouraged when you do encounter a drop in the amount of the trade that you are using.
- Profit – To be able to profit, you will need to make your Forex trade in the time that there is a big rise in the amount that is listed on the Forex trading guide within the London hammer. It is a good idea to try new things and to make sure that you are going to be

able to do different things with the trades. Since you know that the London hammer strategy will eventually come back up, you can always use that to help yourself understand the way that it will be increased. For example, you can buy into the Forex trade when it is really low, knowing that it will come back up. You can then trade again once it has risen up again so that you can profit off of the different things that are happening. It is always a good idea to make the most profit possible so that you can enjoy the experience that comes with Forex trading.

There are many different options that come along with trading and with the different things that are going on in the trades that you do. It is always a good idea to try to figure out the right way to use the London hammer and to make sure that you are getting the highest profits possible for what you want to be able to do with your trades.

Attitude

The way that the London hammer works is that there are rises, falls, and plateaus. Throughout each of these, you need to be careful to leave yourself the opportunity to use these to your advantage. If you don't know what you are doing or that there *will* be problems that come along with your trading, you will not be able to figure out the right way to trade or how it is going to work for you. Always do your best to prepare for the trade and to include all of the different information that you need while you are doing the trades.

Those who are trading Forex will need to be flexible. Since you are going to use the London hammer strategy, you need to be *very* flexible. The flexibility that you have will keep you from having major problems when it comes to the options that are included with your trades. Always work your way into the program and make sure that you are getting the most out of the different types of trades that are available to you. If you want to make sure that you are getting the best experience possible, your attitude with flexibility about the situation is the most important aspect of the trading regime.

Pros

Knowing that you are going to have a price that is going to eventually rise again is one of the best parts of having everything that you need to do with your London hammer strategy. You can make sure that you are getting the best experience possible by keeping that in mind and by allowing yourself the chance to relax when there is a dip in the amount that is created by the London hammer. If you want to get what you can out of the strategy and the trades that you make that are associated with it, you can try new things that will give you the chance to see that the trade can really be profitable.

Another major benefit that comes with the London hammer is that you will always have that guarantee that you are going to have the price rise again. Since there are almost no guarantees in most types of trading and with the majority of strategies that you find, this is a commodity that you can truly benefit from. Once you know what you are doing and you can fit the London hammer into your strategy, you will be able to get the most out of the experience. Have a good understanding of the different things that you can do.

Cons

Perhaps one of the biggest problems that people see with the London hammer is the fluctuation. Most people get worried that their trade amount will not rise again or that they will not be able to get the best amount possible for the trades that they have. When this does happen, it is important to make sure that you are getting the best experience possible. It is a wise decision to try and remember that you will always have a rise in the amount that your trade is worth.

Cons that are also included with your London hammer strategy are things like the initial investment being very high and the risk being large also. If you do not know what you are doing and if you have to try and make things work for yourself, you won't be able to get the best experience possible. If you are trying to get the highest profit possible, you will need to put a lot of money into it.

Since it is risky and it can be hard to get the amount back, this is not the best strategy to use when you are first getting started. Build up some of the capital that you have to spend on your investments first and then invest your money using the London hammer strategy.

No matter what strategy that you have chosen to use, remember that there are certain attitudes that can help you have an easier time with the investments. It is always a good decision to try and make the right choice for your investments. Keep in mind that there will be pros and cons with any investment strategy choice that you make – be sure to choose the right one that aligns with your needs and with the amount of money that you want to make.

Conclusion

Thanks for making it through to the end of *Forex Trading Top 5 Strategies: The Ultimate Guide to Maximize Your Profit and Reduce Risks.* Let's hope it was informative and able to provide you with all of the tools you need to achieve your goals.

The next step is to figure out which strategy is going to work best for you. Figure out what you want to be able to do and then apply that to the benefits and negatives of each of the options that you have. It will help you to have a better time with the trades that you have, so you can make the most amount of money. Forex can be extremely profitable when you know the right way to trade it according to your goals.

Finally, if you found this book useful in any way, a review on Amazon is always appreciated!

Description

Forex is a trade opportunity that many people choose to use so that they can make a lot of money. When you are using Forex as a trade option, you can make big profits only if you know the right way to do it.

The chances are that you already know what Forex is and that trading it can be profitable, but you may not know the many strategies that you can use to trade that money. Some of the strategies that you will find are not exactly in line with good morals and can actually cause you to lose money in the long run. The strategies that are included in this book will help you to make more money, do it the right way and benefit from all of the different aspects of Forex.

Keep in mind that you can do more with trading only if you follow a strategy. The book includes the following:

- Helpful ideas that will make it easier for you to trade
- Benefits that come along with the various types of trade strategies
- Some cons that you will need to look out for with each of the strategies
- The type of attitude that you need to have to be able to succeed with the different strategies
- Specific steps that will have you profiting from the trades that you are doing.

Once you read this book, you will be able to effectively figure out what type of trade you should make, the strategy that you should use to get to that point, and the potential that you have to profit. Each of the chapters of the book focuses on a different types of strategy and is full of information that will help you learn as much as possible about the strategy that you have chosen to learn about.

www.ingramcontent.com/pod-product-compliance
Lightning Source LLC
Chambersburg PA
CBHW071424220526
45469CB00004B/1415